THE SPACE BEYOND

THE SPACE BEYOND

Jo Field

WordAid.org.uk

First published in 2011 for WordAid.org.uk
by Categorical Books
70 Margate Road, Herne Bay, Kent CT6 7BH

For further information about this and other WordAid projects, please visit www.wordaid.org.uk

ISBN 978-1-904662-12-9

A CIP record for this book is available from the British Library

All profits from the sales of this book go to Dementia UK (Registered Charity Number 1039404)

To order more copies, please send a cheque for £7 per copy (including £1 postage & packing) or £12 for two books (£5 per book plus £2 postage and packaging) to Categorical Books at the above address or visit www.wordaid.org.uk

Printed in Great Britain by Lightning Source

Foreword

Old age is a country we all wish to reach. But as ever greater numbers of our loved ones and acquaintances spend increasing amounts of time there, the postcards we receive back become bleaker and bleaker. If, when we're there, we're found to be suffering from any infirmity (including the lack of a large fortune), the prospects for a happy, dignified or even humane sojourn are poor.

In *The Space Beyond* Jo Field charts this territory with characteristic insight. Combining empathy, honesty and humour, her poems track the cultural differences we notice as we cross the frontier into old age and illuminate the often terrifying landscapes of its interior. *The Space Beyond* also examines the power and properties of memory, and the special relationship with the past that we develop as we get older.

All the profits from the sale of *The Space Beyond* go to Dementia UK. This is a charity whose mission is to improve the quality of life for all people affected by dementia. As well as contributing to policy-making and debate, the charity promotes good practice in dementia care, training professionals to work with older people and supporting and developing Admiral Nursing, a specialist service focused on meeting the needs of carers and families. This enables many sufferers of dementia to remain in their own homes for as long as possible, and patients and families to receive the support they need.

If you have found *The Space Beyond* enlightening and enjoyable, then please encourage others to buy and read it. Your support will help those living with dementia now. And whichever side of the border to old age you inhabit, it's a book that may help you prepare for the journey ahead.

Vicky Wilson
WordAid.org.uk

The Things She's Done!

She knows there should be more.
Instead she creeps inside her head
and shuts the door.

Contents

Towards the Sea

Unnoticed by his sullen downcast eye
I pass that four-hundred-year-ancient boy
– rucksack, iPod, morning-showered scent –
still dawdling to school reluctantly.

Abandoning the field where one magpie
picks over summer, climbing the autumn track
I scrape between the brambles – devil-spat –
and beads of hawthorn blood darkened to wine.

A blackbird panics – his staccato cry,
the small-scale swoop of wings – and there's the stench
of something rotting sweetly in the hedge
behind the grizzled beards of traveller's joy.

The earth is stretched like vellum: thin and dry.
Each footfall strikes an echo underground.
The present is dislodged in measured drops
to calcify with other worn-out time.

Wintry up ahead, a flap of sky
hangs white and vacant in the arc of trees.
I know what's waiting in the space beyond:
the blunt edge of the land. And endless sea.

Advent

The un-fathomed growl
and mortar boom
from infinite tons
in tongues of water flung
to the brake
of the sea wall.
The foamflakes' icy kiss.
The glowering rise
in a jagged rank
like snow-stacked northern pines
to tower and hang.
The fold, collapse
and tumble and fall,
smash and smatter and hiss.
And again, again
the kraken's roar.

Not Young

Today, perhaps you woke to find
that overnight
all this *old* stuff –
until now just gradually gaining ground –
had put on a spurt,
entirely engulfed your muscles,
lagged your bones.
You nursed a brain
slumped heavy in its skull,
old and tired.
Your crabbed old feet, leather
in leather, set about
their tired old path.
The day waxed
old before its time.
Even the sun looked every one
of its four and a half billion years,
heaving wanly up the sky.
Maybe you reflected
that someone as old as you
should at least be wise,
all-seeing? All you see
is your long long life
tumbled like the chaos
in the wake of a tornado.
And blood welling
from hindsight
sharp
as a stiletto.

Refurbishment

Dust off the vacuum cleaner. Dig out that crevice tool.
Convolutions must be eased apart with care,
suction applied precisely along their length
to clear away the fluff.

If the cerebellum is a little musty
treat it with a fungicide – research online,
and Google *fillers* to be squeezed between the lobes.

Plaster over things you're not quite sure about
then sand down any roughness
in the beta wave.

Sweep up debris and discard in bin-liners,
tying them tightly for the dustmen's sake.
Both hemispheres should be well washed
with mild detergent.

Choose a colour you can live with: not too dull
nor over-bright – something in keeping with the character.
Apply it in two generous layers
to the thalamus.

Mix paste. Opt for the Extra Strong stuff to avoid
slippage and peeling. Retrieve those old Reminders
from oblivion. Paper the cortex with them. Leftover scraps
may be employed to cheer up alpha rhythms
with some découpage.

When you've finished, sit back. Feel
the benefits. Revel in your handiwork.
Don't dwell on the inevitable flaws.
Don't start to ponder
the wisdom of your DIY. Remember:
this is a period structure. If you're fortunate,
irregularities will be excused
as part of its appeal.

Clock Work

Do you drag ex-homes behind like a crocodile tail?
Inventories of valance and meat-safe,
glory-hole, peeled linoleum and ceiling cracks,
the swelling curtains, windows wide for waiting at,
the wallpaper flowers, the picture rails.

Is each house riddled with mile-long corridors
shining in blurs of ghost-mote dust?
From every corner
does something instantly familiar call?
Do children clatter and hoot, lost boys
and girls who can't grow up? Do
those other lives of yours still run, but
interrupted like the track of a snail
or that broken line down the centre of the street?

Are you forever listening, ears strained to aching point,
for the *tick-tick* of the past as it's snapping
at your heels?

Sliding on Ice

I catch myself
doing that old-lady thing with the fingers
sticking them rigid at unlikely angles
in a concentrated effort
of balance and
I slither brakeless through
a magician's long cabinet of knives
arms flailing hands nails
snagging tearing
scrabbling for a hold.

Gathering speed the soles
of my boots begin to shred,
electric shocks of hair
frazzle hoar-stiff,
breath
like dry ice
glues frigid lips
in a snarl
to smarting teeth
as I chute on
trailing ribbons
of leather
and blood,
the roar
of the crowd
just
a glockenspiel
thrill in
the icicled cave
of my
ear.

My Dead

Going back over the snow
I squint out against blinding cold
above rumps and flanks jogging,
shoulders straining in the traces
and those heavy-branched heads.

When I see you half-buried to the west
I haul on the reins,
bring the whole equipage to a halt
with a tossing of antlers, scudding
of runners biting into ice.

My boots sink with every pace
in the hollow of places I've trodden before.
I kneel to scoop and scrape and brush
at grains and crystals clinging,
until you must be nearly free.

Limbs were abandoned just so, one foot
turned as if mid-trot. Your trunk's flung
in a soundless bellow, an ear flat
to your neck, your mantle of petrified skin
sculpted on muscle and bone.

You've lain here unmoved for tens of thousands of years.
I'm drawn to your side again
and again – these visits
too lonely even for tears.

Rest of My Life

I can't make out if he was ninety, or a hundred, or
a hundred and ten, but I'm sitting on *Bill Swinton*'s bench
under a flat pan of milky sky, the air
choked with the comfortable sound of pigeons
burbling into mobile phones: *I'm on the post . . .*
I'm on the wire . . . And I'm dragging
on the early heat of the sun already high, the towering scent
of grasses woven in yarrow and scabious,
the distant firefly antics of the sea, as if
on a last cigarette.

Walking home under the shade of elders, the lower wood –
lively in dim and bright – teases through tall slats of its retaining
fence
like a mystical flicker-book, and I'm thinking:
if every morning were like this, then
it mightn't be so terrible after all to live to ninety, or a hundred,
or even a hundred and ten.

Running on Rails

You were off on a trip to the seaside, all of you
packed in a first-class compartment, snug
and self-contained, with sandwiches,
shrimping nets, waterwings, plans
for the castles you'd build,
your songs and squabblings.

Your mother got off at the wrong stop.
Dad couldn't hold her. She struggled down
leaving her bags abandoned on the rack,
never waved to you craning from the window.
Only the engine's shrill elastic whistle stretched and stretched
between you and her stillness dwindling.

The rest of you dispersed
through the crowded pitch and toss
of second class.
In the window's grime you scratched
sketches of the bucket and spade you'd lost.

Searching the aisles
    of staggered seats
for a congenial face,
    you wrenched doors wide,
shoved them shut,
    matched your lurch
to the ratchet and hitch
    of the wheels.

The train crawled into run-down stations,
settled at each with a sigh.
You noticed your father get out
carrying his dog-eared suitcase
of ancient holiday clothes.
Leaning your head on the seat-back's stubble
you watch through shuttered eyes
as passengers come and go.
Outside the doors, their weight of metal slams
piling like scrap-heaps,
hover the station's thin gull-cries.

Is this the train for the coast?
You meet with blank looks
until the guard comes round
to seal your fate.
It is the wrong train after all,
one that will chunter just as far as the next stop,
where it terminates.

Planets Past

Night muscles in like treacle through a ragged hole,
with the odd planet snagged on splinters.
Of course they're all called Past, you can tell

by glancing at them, some of them eternal winter,
others nothing but summer, golden
and rosy and attractively dimpled.

Why, drifting helpless in the memory doldrums,
is it the mizzly planets which draw the eye?
You'd think it would recoil from coldness,

from shivers engendered there. Then why
must it persist in firing up, towing
the mind behind it through the soupy sky

to touch down flump on an unwelcoming
world you hoped you'd long ago forgotten?
Why won't it land you in a place of singing

and lightness where you'd recognise the pattern
of joy that's woven in the stars,
where you'd be glad to be abandoned, not on

some wallowing asteroid? Why are you mostly cast
away to flounder on the bleakest of the planets Past?

Another Empty Box

Listen to the wind. It sucks the force
from a life that lingers, lost in all but name.
The past, packed neatly in a bottom drawer –
laid in, laid up, laid out in tissue –
is invaded. Raw wind
insinuates through wormholes, blasts
it all apart.
        There's nothing left.
Only the shadow of eventful years
is spewed in ribbons on the gale's breath.

Wind claws the eyes and wrings them dry of tears.
The weather man assures us spring will come,
but in the newspaper's clairvoyant squares
there are no suns –
just clouds that cluster at the fag end of a winter far too long.

Afterlife

Painted Glass

The more you look the more you see.
Too many angels to count – milky,
opalescent as the sad eyes of the old,
each one the symbol of some compromised belief.
Swirls and flecks of gold,
flash of red, dashes of blue:
lapis, cobalt, aquamarine,
little heavens pushing their way through –
and wing on terrifying wing towering to the apogee.

Funeral Rites

At the priest's feet the women weep.
A magnetic box weighs heavy on the eye.
Inside lies, we presume,
the rest of you, abandoned as it was
by faith, by reason, hope and heart.
We have cobbled a kind of history to see you out
and he who might have helped the living
stands apart, recites it as he lights the fuse
to send you on your way.

Division of Spoils

Raking the ashes, we find
tumbled from the conveyor belt of life
things which once were precious:
albums of foreign photographs, knives
with pale bone handles,
two clocks, a sleeping mandolin
and scores of geometric implements
in walnut cases plumped with purple velvet.

We'll hitch them loosely
like tin cans to a wedding car,
trail them in our wake.
Sooner or later we'll forget
just where they came from,
as if we ever knew.

Envoi

The drive home is eternal. In the dusk
on every branch and spur of lay-by
pantechnicons are gathering to roost.

Failures with a Hand Camera

Scenes from a grandmother's album

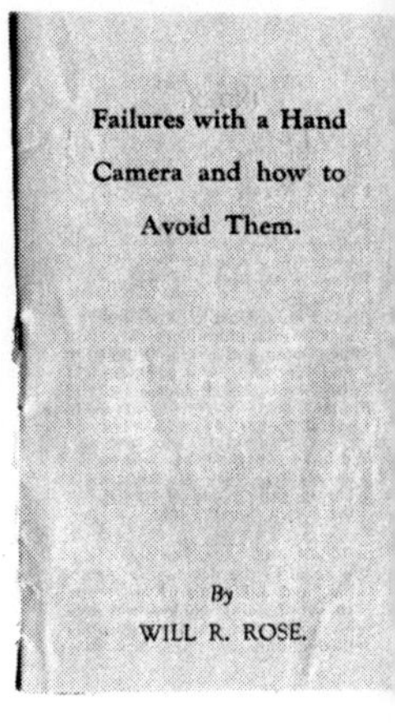
Failures with a Hand Camera and how to Avoid Them.

By

WILL R. ROSE.

I. Under Exposure

Even if the sun is shining in the open,
snapshots must not be taken
in the shadow of trees, houses, etc.

But a Mrs Porter – defiant
in a drab black length of coat, her stiff arms
clutching a grey sheaf of flowers –
has taken root under a hedge
that's much too tall.
A nervous smile
and eyes brim full of dark
are circled by the shady halo of her hat.
For countless years
she's been abandoned in the garden,
stolid on her single gleaming boot.

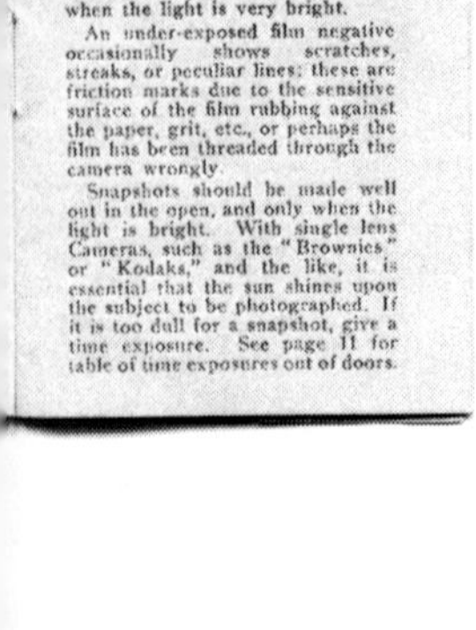

1

UNDER EXPOSURE.

A certain amount of light is necessary to produce a good negative, and if snapshots are taken with ordinary Cameras in a dull light the results are disappointing, and generally failures.

Even if the sun is shining in the open, snapshots must not be taken in the shadow of trees, houses, etc., or in a room. The largest stop should always be used, except when the light is very bright.

An under-exposed film negative occasionally shows scratches, streaks, or peculiar lines; these are friction marks due to the sensitive surface of the film rubbing against the paper, grit, etc., or perhaps the film has been threaded through the camera wrongly.

Snapshots should be made well out in the open, and only when the light is bright. With single lens Cameras, such as the "Brownies," or "Kodaks," and the like, it is essential that the sun shines upon the subject to be photographed. If it is too dull for a snapshot, give a time exposure. See page 11 for table of time exposures out of doors.

II. Over Exposure

The shutter should not have been open nearly so long.

It's 1905. Self is about to bathe.
Unfazed by the absence of any kind of weather
she leans precarious from the perpendicular
where a pallid rocky beach trails to a paler sea.
The lily-whiteness of her dressing gown is gathered loosely
to reveal a swimming costume – neck to daring knee.
Don't look too closely at the youthful face
in case you might discover
that old woman, never to be,
waiting still in vain behind the eyes.

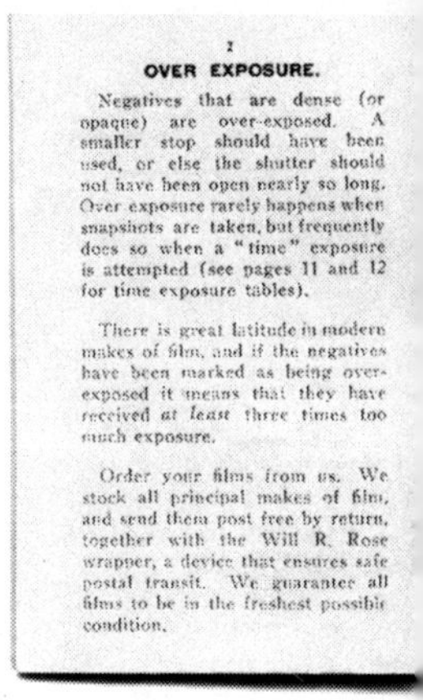

7

OVER EXPOSURE.

Negatives that are dense (or opaque) are over-exposed. A smaller stop should have been used, or else the shutter should not have been open nearly so long. Over exposure rarely happens when snapshots are taken, but frequently does so when a "time" exposure is attempted (see pages 11 and 12 for time exposure tables).

There is great latitude in modern makes of film, and if the negatives have been marked as being over-exposed it means that they have received *at least* three times too much exposure.

Order your films from us. We stock all principal makes of film, and send them post free by return, together with the Will R. Rose wrapper, a device that ensures safe postal transit. We guarantee all films to be in the freshest possible condition.

III. Blurred Negatives

Never jerk the camera. In fact
the trigger should be released
as one would fire a revolver or a gun.

The war is ended that will end all wars . . .
Bob's out of uniform and skipping on the lawn,
legs a skirl of movement, picking up
his young wife's laughter where he'd left it.
Even as we smile indulgently
his nimble feet are hobbled, chained
to our crystal ball, where looms a future
so obviously fragile now it's past.

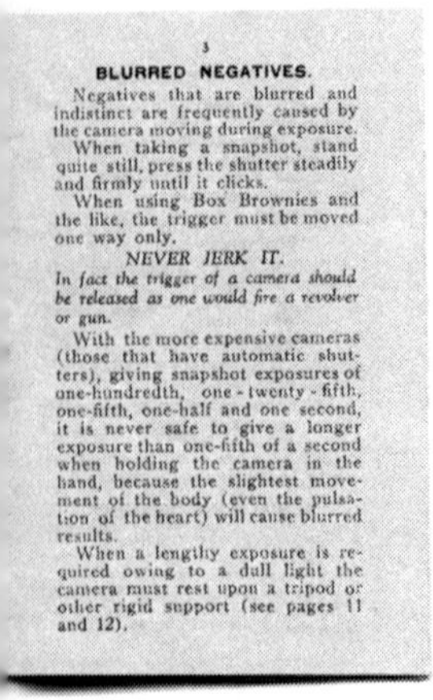

3

BLURRED NEGATIVES.

Negatives that are blurred and indistinct are frequently caused by the camera moving during exposure.

When taking a snapshot, stand quite still, press the shutter steadily and firmly until it clicks.

When using Box Brownies and the like, the trigger must be moved one way only.

NEVER JERK IT.

In fact the trigger of a camera should be released as one would fire a revolver or gun.

With the more expensive cameras (those that have automatic shutters), giving snapshot exposures of one-hundredth, one-twenty-fifth, one-fifth, one-half and one second, it is never safe to give a longer exposure than one-fifth of a second when holding the camera in the hand, because the slightest movement of the body (even the pulsation of the heart) will cause blurred results.

When a lengthy exposure is required owing to a dull light the camera must rest upon a tripod or other rigid support (see pages 11 and 12).

IV. Fogged Negatives

Light has affected the film.
Was there a hole in the bellows?

All's well.
Bob's sixteen again. Propped
against a woolly bag of golf clubs
he's drained bloodless by the strain
of shielding the years to come
securely in his fist. It's jammed
deep in the baggy pocket of a blazer
that's been laundered of its substance.
On his ashen hair a cap's pushed back
to show, already, his son's face
crowding the scrubbed oval of his own.

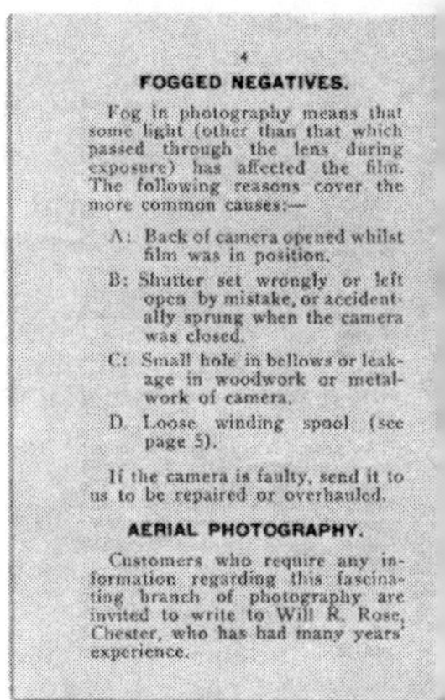
4

FOGGED NEGATIVES.

Fog in photography means that some light (other than that which passed through the lens during exposure) has affected the film. The following reasons cover the more common causes:—

A: Back of camera opened whilst film was in position.

B: Shutter set wrongly or left open by mistake, or accidentally sprung when the camera was closed.

C: Small hole in bellows or leakage in woodwork or metalwork of camera.

D. Loose winding spool (see page 5).

If the camera is faulty, send it to us to be repaired or overhauled.

AERIAL PHOTOGRAPHY.

Customers who require any information regarding this fascinating branch of photography are invited to write to Will R. Rose, Chester, who has had many years' experience.

V. Film Winding Difficulties

Wind slowly. There will be less risk
of passing the numbers in the window.

The numbers here are random –
1917. 1904. 1921 . . .
Then spool too quickly until 1865.
We've passed worlds of obscurity
to happen upon Mother, book in hand,
perched before heavy curtains and Greek keys.
A tasselled couch supports her studio pose,
while she herself is weighed down, lost
in plump wood-pigeon disguise.

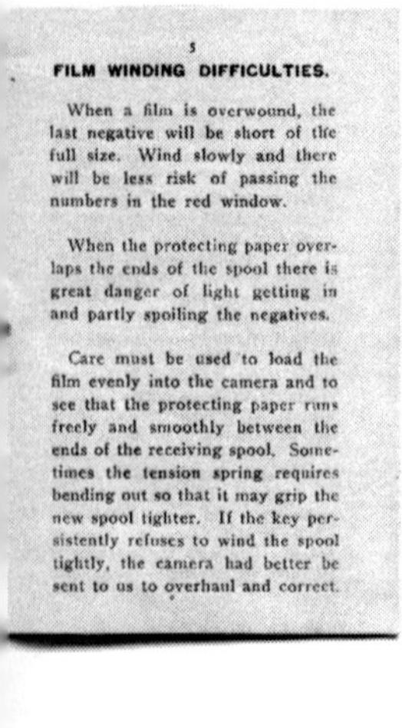

5

FILM WINDING DIFFICULTIES.

When a film is overwound, the last negative will be short of the full size. Wind slowly and there will be less risk of passing the numbers in the red window.

When the protecting paper overlaps the ends of the spool there is great danger of light getting in and partly spoiling the negatives.

Care must be used to load the film evenly into the camera and to see that the protecting paper runs freely and smoothly between the ends of the receiving spool. Sometimes the tension spring requires bending out so that it may grip the new spool tighter. If the key persistently refuses to wind the spool tightly, the camera had better be sent to us to overhaul and correct.

VI. The Finder

The finder of folding cameras
is frequently the cause of cutting off
a portion of the picture.

Binkie, West Highland canine,
hero of a dozen snaps,
dances on short back legs,
receiving dinner from a woman
who stoops, benevolent
although she has no head.
Across the page, and looming large
in its solidity,
the tomb of Timothy William glares.
Only the pencilled caption-dates lay bare
his mayfly history.

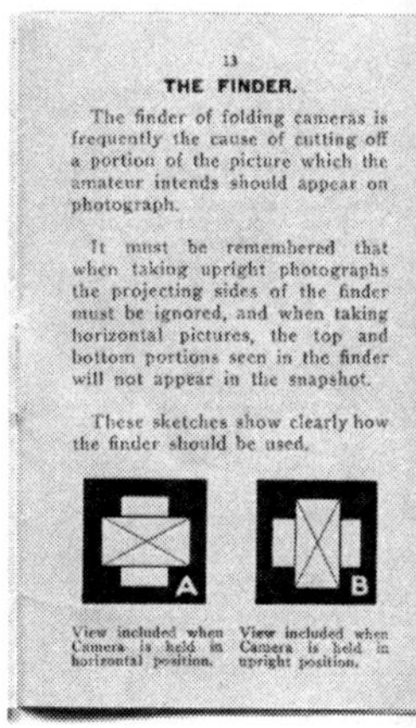
13

THE FINDER.

The finder of folding cameras is frequently the cause of cutting off a portion of the picture which the amateur intends should appear on photograph.

It must be remembered that when taking upright photographs the projecting sides of the finder must be ignored, and when taking horizontal pictures, the top and bottom portions seen in the finder will not appear in the snapshot.

These sketches show clearly how the finder should be used.

View included when Camera is held in horizontal position.

View included when Camera is held in upright position.

VII. Indistinct Negatives

It is necessary to have the subject
placed at least 12 feet away.

Aunt Fan's home is a ghost house,
bleached and faded and far,
lodging phantom dolls
all bled to dryness by oblivion.
Steps, picked out in frigid light,
stack up to a veranda
and a little figure frozen to the rail.
It's saluting in the distance
above the scrapes of marram grass
like scratches on a plate,
to another, clearer picture
where the true Aunt Fan
sits distinctly on a hewn-out log.
A hat collapses sadly on the gravel
as she aims her sternly level gaze
straight through us to eternity.

6

INDISTINCT NEGATIVES.

When using fixed focus cameras, such as No. 2 or No. 3 "Brownies," or the like, it is necessary to have the subject to be photographed placed at least 12 feet away. The lenses in these cameras are so fixed that all objects beyond 12 feet and up to infinity are in focus. If the subject photographed is nearer to the camera than 12 feet the picture is indistinct. If, however, it is required to photograph an object nearer to the camera than 12 feet, a portrait attachment should be used. A portrait attachment is an additional lens, which can be instantly fixed to the front of the camera and enables one to take sharp pictures as near as five or six feet. The cost is a very small one, and they double the efficiency of the camera. They do not interfere with the working at all, and we strongly recommend them.

VIII. Errors in Judging Distance

A good way of measuring is to pace it,
reckoning one fair stride as three feet.

Here's Anne, achieving her first steps
in a time that's been erased.
Beneath a face round as a saucer,
a body chunked with swaddle,
her bonsai legs are neatly socked and shod
and coping well. For how robust she is!
And jolly – marching forward
confident and safe into the sun,
led by the hand of the only arm
of some one-legged man
to where the shadow of her mother's head
is lying on the ground.

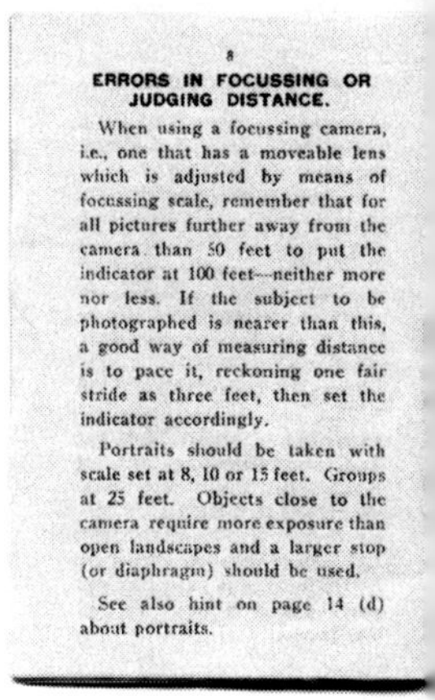
8

ERRORS IN FOCUSSING OR JUDGING DISTANCE.

When using a focussing camera, i.e., one that has a moveable lens which is adjusted by means of focussing scale, remember that for all pictures further away from the camera than 50 feet to put the indicator at 100 feet—neither more nor less. If the subject to be photographed is nearer than this, a good way of measuring distance is to pace it, reckoning one fair stride as three feet, then set the indicator accordingly.

Portraits should be taken with scale set at 8, 10 or 15 feet. Groups at 25 feet. Objects close to the camera require more exposure than open landscapes and a larger stop (or diaphragm) should be used.

See also hint on page 14 (d) about portraits.

IX. General Remarks

A misty lens gives a misty picture.

We wonder at their equanimity,
these foreigners –
so rugged yet so delicate –
who seize the present as the only place to be.
If we insist on buffing off the dust,
burning to shed light on those secret lives,
how can we fail to ignite the pyres
of trust and expectation in their eyes.

14

GENERAL REMARKS.

(a) Study the instruction book which is given with each camera.

(b) Clean the lens occasionally with a linen handkerchief. A misty lens gives misty pictures.

(c) Be careful to keep the fingers from the front of the lens when making the exposure, and also (with folding cameras) do not touch the bellows. Many negatives are spoiled by these means, through being partially obscured.

(d) When taking portraits in Sunlight, arrange your subjects so that the light falls sideways on the face and not full in the eyes; much better "likenesses" will thus be obtained.

(e) Try to avoid having the sun shining full into the lens when taking a photograph.

(f) Dust-specks occasionally show on the negatives.

The inside of the camera should be wiped out with a damp cloth from time to time.

(g) See that such fixed focus folding cameras as the V.P.K.'s, etc., are fully extended when a snap is taken, otherwise the picture will be blurred and spoilt.

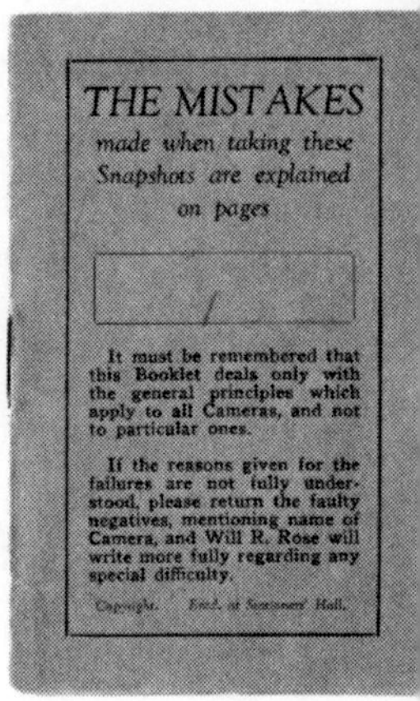

THE MISTAKES

made when taking these Snapshots are explained on pages

It must be remembered that this Booklet deals only with the general principles which apply to all Cameras, and not to particular ones.

If the reasons given for the failures are not fully understood, please return the faulty negatives, mentioning name of Camera, and Will R. Rose will write more fully regarding any special difficulty.

Copyright. Entd. at Stationers' Hall.

Their Remains

One grandfather

listened to his mother-in-law when she told
of Irish unrest, of exile to England;

grieved at the untimely death of his wife so that never again
was she mentioned in front of her children;

had a hand in the engineering of railways in India;
sketched locomotives, perfect Bagnalls, for his son;

banished that same pale boy to the dog basket
for biting his sister;

every morning, totted up the ages
of the clothes he wore, working from inner to outer;
refused to leave the house until they totalled
more than one hundred years;

licked an index finger, held it against the wind
to determine which route he'd walk each day.

One grandfather

half a world away
had heard his grandmother speak
of a rough voyage from England;

embarrassed his future wife with an engagement ring
like something from a cracker
(which it was), producing the real one later with a flourish;

turned his hand to most things,
from sheep-dealing and shearing to embroidery

to catching shit from a polo pony
brought indoors, before it could hit the carpet;

was fond of fancy dress;

donned a turban to fool fellow-travellers
on a sub-continental train
with invitations to a non-existent dining car.

Ring Out Ye Bells

Every couple of years
Gran brought her billycan to stay and
her double chins, her black hats
and alien games and
her dresses worn inside out,
messes of seam and label and
flapping shoulder-pads and wild threads exposed
and her hairnets spun by spiders and
invisible hairpins that you'd keep seeing
about the house after she'd gone
where they'd slid from her fine white hair as
she brandished her ear trumpet, ivory and leather
loud with what-did-you-says and
passed on messages for my mother from
across the ocean and
new books for me, adventures
of kookaburras and
Norah of Billabong and wallabies and
when my parents took their gymshoes and
went off to Scottish Dancing
the lusty duets the two of us bawled,
singing with gusto about
making love to the ladies and
Ring Archie Bells.

The Past Is a Disaster

Everyone in it is dead.
You're the prince, battling
through thorns after a hundred years,
happening on strangers – nothing
but empty attitudes struck – and a dog
which used to welcome you from school
stretched mat-flat.

In the atrium
a half-recalled acquaintance sprawls on stones.
An old friend lies, eyes mirroring the vacant sky
and nothing else.
Floating in a leaf-choked pool, others you knew –
all offering up their silent smirks.

You tiptoe on mosaics
through marble columns in the peristyle
where a grandparent decomposes –
accoutrements of song and fairy tale
spilling among roses.
You climb on crumbling plinths
to where your mother and your father sit.

Your lips, blood pulsing,
cling to her cold forehead,
his frozen cheek.
But they won't wake.

Mantel Piece

At first she'll tread carefully, high
on the gnarled balls of her feet like a dancer
or a cat,
right arm crammed between one bony flank
and the wall,
knuckles like galls pressed to her thigh,
the fingers spidering.
Her left arm she'll extend in space,
graceful
as she steps over china dogs and candlesticks,
frames stuffed with babies, weddings, graduations.

But she might pause,
turn
to face the room, feet flat, toes stiff-
curled, clinging to the edge, palms of her hands –
their lines of life and fate, mounts of Venus and the moon –
spreadeagled against pink cabbage roses
printed on the chimney breast.

Then she'll shuffle crabwise, not bothering any more
about knickknacks dislodged –
mementoes gathered over all the years
only to topple, spiral in slow-motion
down to the tiles beneath. Either way
she will no longer care:

if she launches to dip and swoop
past the standard lamp, over the nest of polished tables,
between nets lapping and shifting like tides
and out through the window thrust open to the sky,
she won't care.

Or if she should fall

Losing

She asks me if I've brought her cigarettes.
She's never smoked, but these days she forgets.

Long minutes, hours, weeks will pass her by.
She breathes. She sobs. She shouts. And she forgets.

She can't remember where she is, or why.
I tell her constantly but she forgets.

Her world's a static round of repetition:
she eats, she sits, she sleeps, and she forgets.

I watch her in the throes of demolition –
remind her that I love her. She forgets.

Each day more bits of her break off and die.
I hold her, croon our song. Still she forgets.

She doesn't know me sometimes, turns all shy
as if we might have met, but she forgets.

Sixty years together. No regrets . . .
although that whole life's lost now she forgets.

Slidoffad

Because he had disgraced himself again
his mother pushed him roughly back home,
their progress snagged on ragged paving slabs.
The perambulator rattled those soft bones
while the sound of her displeasure battered his ears
like raucous black birds flying round his head.
Uncomprehending, yet he registered humiliation.
Somehow still
whenever he sees daffodils, something is triggered
like a small electric shock, somewhere
in the frayed wiring of his brain: something
NOW.

Now,
afraid in the mire of his brain, something –
like that small electric shock somewhere
whenever he sees daffodils – something is triggered
somehow still.
Uncomprehending, yet he registers humiliation
like raucous black birds flying round his head
while the sound of her displeasure batters his ears,
the wheelchair rattles those brittle bones.
Their progress snagged on ragged paving slabs,
his daughter pushes him roughly back to the Home
because he has disgraced himself again.

Sunflowers

A congregation
uniformed for worship,
rank on flaming yellow rank.

A ragged conflagration,
a kaleidoscope twist
on the theme of their star,

all heads turning, burning
leisurely through each gold day
from east to west.

These amputated few,
forced to waste their final hours
in water and glass

backs to the beckoning sun,
paralysed,
can only feel it pass.

Marooned on Ithaca

Give them soft beds to lie on after a soothing bath,
and feed them well. The ancients knew
the proper way to use an aged body.
But what of the antique inner man
whose itchy feet kick feebly in their slippers?

As though to breathe were life!

Laertes, cast a world away from town,
is anchored in his orchard.
He stoops and scratches at the ground,
snatches the earth in both his hands
to offer up a supplication to the gods,
letting the black dust pour on to his ashy head.

As though to breathe were life.

His much-enduring son perhaps won't shout at him for that,
not shake him by the shoulders.
The same son who, steering well clear for twenty years,
abandoned him to lonely battle with his muddled brain,
sent no Calypso to while away the father's twilight
as he mouldered, with rumours of a shroud
constantly re-woven, willing him dead.

As though to breathe were life!

The lungs still heave, still bellow – pulling threads of air
through nostrils, pushing them out again. Blood
navigates the heart, wine's mixed to ease the mind, bread
travels to the stomach, bladder and bowel perform
a semblance of their role . . . Sleep

eludes him. Waking dreams wash to and fro between the Scylla
and Charybdis of his memory.
Spent muscles flex behind a shield. A spear is primed.
But in the eye, that knife-edge glint is only the whimper of his
soul.

As though to breathe were life.

You'd think Odysseus at least might understand.

To a Dog

after Yeats

When you are old and slothful, dull and fat
and snoring by the fire, your muzzle white,
but in your dreams you're spoiling for a fight
and, dreaming, you still chase the neighbour's cat.

While life is comfortable and you are King
dream easy, undisturbed by any fears
about the progress of advancing years
and what the coming weeks and months may bring.

It's only we who are obliged to flog
a dead-horse life, are forced to struggle on
when dignity and faculties are gone.
Sleep well. We wouldn't do it to a dog.

Beggarman Thief

Life? It's chewed you up and spat you out.
You're inconvenient, uncomfortable, nothing
but a number – a disposable tool
in the box of party politics.
A tinker, were you? A tailor? Who knows?
Decency always been your rule? No longer.
You're a pain in the neck
like that persistent war-wound
which nobody asks about.
Sea legs, steady through years on deck,
have let you down. You're washed up
on the shifting sands of a land that's dry
and crumbling as your skin.
A rich life, was it? Who cares?
Not the inscrutable ones
with reckless governance over this end of it.
Poor man, forced to plead,
to steal each vexed piece of attention
by means of any disconcerting trick.
No wonder there's relief all round
on one of those mornings
when a single knife-beam slicing from the cloud
points like the finger of God,
and another stone is counted out.

Castaway

Because
you can't do it for yourself darlin'
remember?

She doesn't remember. Sinks down the chair
like a bob of lead, her bones of coral
papered with jellyfish stings.
Eyes surface, swimming in stout glass shells,
fasten a pearly glare. She's seized
by ebb tides, champs a vague salt tang of dread.
It's there on the horizon, always. Always a blur.
She strikes out from the shore, is washed
back again. Her mind's the one that got away.
They've let it go, those aliens
who pull on rubber gloves
and waggle oarweed fingers as they come.

kerPOW

Somewhere in a kitchen near you
a Superhero sits,
the sharp bones of his backside planted
in the vinyl seat of a beechwood chair.
On a Formica table-top his shopping waits.

Probably he's looking at his hands, turning them
– palm up, palm down – to marvel
at ridges like corrugated cardboard on their nails,
their trout-back liver-spots, burled veins
and the pinches of shrivelled plastic skin.

He'll be remembering when these same hands –
he's almost sure these are the ones – would reach
to halt the fall of screaming bodies from great heights,
find finger-holds to swarm him up sheer walls,
biff villains with their casual balled-up fists.

Now he's cursing as he jabs and hacks with knives,
spoon-handles, skewers – beating off spills,
parrying sprung leaks – desperate to break in
to cartons, packets, intractable jars and tins –
trying to fight his way into a paper bag.

Dark Flow

As a child he was huge,
flaming in the universe like the first sun.
His laughing mouth gulped planets,
fingers grasped whole skeins of cloud.
When he danced, the stars throbbed hot,
moons boiled around his head.

As he grew, somehow
he dwindled.
Concentric ripples of his cosmos, instead
of spreading wider still
pulled slowly tight together – a snail
hugging itself into its shell, curled
to the tiny brittle womb
of his ending.

On Hold

He missed the evening flight, she's gone ahead without him.
    With a static queue
that snakes around the hours he's held up at check-in.

Towing the suitcase which he packed himself, its hoarded weight
    bumping his heels,
he shuffles to the desk, watches the shake

of his hands fumbling passport and tickets. Luggage tagged
    like all the rest,
reluctantly he lets it go. Time settles down to drag.

Trapped in the departure lounge he's conscious of the dark
    beyond the glass –
its lumbering slow monsters, quicksilver shocks

of light. He should be joining her. Stifled in a pall
    of empty space
he's sitting out the night until his number's called.

Skin

We don't leave the light on any more
and we take it slow, tantric.

If you're measuring pleasure
it's the fingers these days which give

and take the most as they travel
the rollers and troughs of this

the largest organ.
Sixty-odd years since we two virgins

cast off together, startled and star-struck
by the newness of the other,

its alien complexities, its concaves
where convexities might be, its

unexpected hards and softs.
Now there's untold solace in tracing

the progress of each sag and crease
when, as if to dope a biplane,

the hand smoothes and varnishes
places where skin fits over bone,

or it animates flesh hanging
folded like the wasted wings of the moa.

No more the fervour of discovery –
it's the same secret island

only, a simoom is blowing, dry
and dusty, re-forming contours

into a comfortable approximation
of how the land once used to lie.

A Pillbox

The squat concrete of it,
unpromising among brambles.
Inside – just the two of us – that
daring secret thrill of happiness.

The small cylindrical hat, yellow
as sunshine. Its wiry froth of veiling.
One scrap of pink paper caught up,
brushed off. His careful fingers.

But not this. Not this affair
of miniature compartments,
pop-up lids and colour-coding.
All this muddle and mortification.

Dandy-Rigged

Every day the old ships limp about the town,
becalmed at corners, tacking on pavements,
signalling with the brave flourish of pennants
in drab blues and buffs, audacious reds.

There's the tartan, her lateen bowsed rakishly;
the broad beam, deep draught of the galleass;
curved stems of caravels; the brigantines;
small cutters, clinker-built, with dipping lugs.

When my vessel's holed and little more than ribs
I hope to find that very brand of courage
to make me leave my hammock, tackle another voyage;
the strength to wrestle with the mizzen-mast,
feet braced, cramped hands raw and cracked
struggling to heft it, step it forward of the transom,
crooking the cold iron of the tiller round its girth.

Let me sheet my leg-o'mutton dandy to an outrigger,
numb fingers working bend and hitch and bowline,
trim the patched canvas when it bells and tugs
and set my face towards the open sea.

Biography

Jo Field's poems have appeared in many publications including *Envoi*, *Equinox*, *Quattrocento*, *Lighten Up Online* and *Release* (the magazine of CAPS, the Captive Animals' Protection Society). They have also featured in anthologies: *Between the Lines* (Stubborn Mule Books, 2008); *Canterbury Poet of the Year* (Canterbury Festival, 2010); *Bugged: Writings from Overhearings* (Bugged, 2010); *Did I Tell You? 131 Poems for Children in Need* (WordAid.org.uk, 2010) and *On the Line* (Canterbury City Press, 2010) as well as in several from Deal Writers.

'Skin' was the winner of the SaveAs Poetry Competition 2009; 'Towards the Sea' came third in the same competition and 'Rest of My Life' was shortlisted.

According to a recent survey conducted at the University of Kent which discovered that 'the average Briton' believes old age starts at 58, Jo Field has already been old for some years. While still granted the flexibility to do so, she is keeping her fingers crossed that things aren't about to get a whole lot worse . . .

Lightning Source UK Ltd.
Milton Keynes UK
13 January 2011

165645UK00001B/3/P

9 781904 662129